COMPREHENSIVE GUIDE TO PERSONAL CYBERSECURITY

Personal Cybersecurity Practices for a Safer Digital Life

Rick Spair

CONTENTS

Introduction

Welcome to this comprehensive guide to personal cybersecurity. As we navigate our lives in an increasingly digital world, cybersecurity has become a paramount concern. Each click, share, and download carries potential risk, and thus understanding how to protect ourselves online is critical.

This guide provides an in-depth exploration of personal cybersecurity, designed to give you the knowledge, tools, and confidence needed to safely navigate the digital landscape. Over the next ten chapters, we'll delve into the many facets of cybersecurity, offering practical tips, recommendations, and strategies to bolster your defenses and keep your personal information safe from cyber threats.

In Chapter 1, we'll begin by demystifying the concept of cybersecurity. This foundational understanding will establish a basis for the more complex topics we'll address later.

Next, in Chapter 2, we'll discuss the creation and management of strong passwords. Passwords are your first line of defense against cyber threats, and learning how to create robust, uncrackable codes is a vital skill.

Chapter 3 focuses on secure web browsing. You'll learn how to identify secure websites, the importance of HTTPS, and tips for safe downloading and browsing.

In Chapter 4, we delve into email security, where we'll discuss phishing, spam, and ways to ensure your communications remain private and secure.

Chapter 5 addresses social media safety. Given the sheer volume of information exchanged on social media, understanding the associated risks and mitigation strategies is crucial.

Chapter 6 covers mobile device security. With smartphones essentially acting as pocket-sized computers, ensuring their safety is paramount.

Chapter 7 centers on protecting personal data. We'll explore data encryption, secure storage, and safe disposal of digital data and devices.

In Chapter 8, we turn our attention to safe online shopping practices. We'll discuss how to identify secure e-commerce sites, safe payment methods, and strategies to protect your financial data.

Chapter 9 focuses on understanding and using antivirus software. Antivirus software is a key tool in your cybersecurity arsenal, and we'll guide you on how to use it effectively.

Finally, in Chapter 10, we bring everything together and guide you in creating a comprehensive personal cybersecurity plan. This plan will help you maintain a robust defense against ongoing and emerging threats.

By the end of this guide, you should have a comprehensive understanding of personal cybersecurity. With this knowledge, you can make informed decisions about your online activities, use digital technology safely and confidently, and protect your digital life from potential threats.

This journey into personal cybersecurity begins with understanding what cybersecurity is and why it matters. Let's dive into our first chapter: Understanding Cybersecurity.

Chapter 1: Understanding Cybersecurity

In the digital age, the importance of understanding cybersecurity cannot be overstated. With the increasing sophistication of cyber threats, it is critical to familiarize oneself with the concept of cybersecurity and its myriad of components. This chapter will serve as an introduction to cybersecurity, focusing on the types of threats, potential consequences of a breach, and the significance of maintaining personal cybersecurity.

What is Cybersecurity?

Cybersecurity refers to the practice of defending computers, servers, mobile devices, electronic systems, networks, and data from digital attacks. These digital attacks are often referred to as cyber-attacks. Cybersecurity can also be termed as information technology security or electronic information security, depending on the context. The overarching goal of cybersecurity is to provide a good security posture for computers and servers, networks, and the data that is stored and transferred.

Types of Cyber Threats

Understanding the diverse array of cyber threats is the first step towards protecting yourself in the digital world. Here are some common types of cyber threats:

Malware: This is a broad term that refers to software designed to harm or exploit any computing device or network. It includes viruses, worms, ransomware, and spyware. Malware can delete or steal data, monitor user activity without consent, or completely take over a device.

Phishing: Phishing is a cybercrime in which targets are contacted by email, telephone, or text message by someone posing as a legitimate institution to lure individuals into providing sensitive data.

Man-in-the-Middle Attack (MitM): This occurs when attackers secretly intercept and potentially alter the communication between two parties who believe they are directly communicating with each other.

SQL Injection: An SQL injection happens when an attacker uses malicious code to manipulate your database into revealing information.

Denial-of-Service (DoS) and Distributed Denial-of-Service (DDoS) Attacks: These attacks overwhelm a system's resources, causing it to become unavailable to users.

The Consequences of a Cybersecurity Breach

The potential consequences of a cybersecurity breach can be severe, particularly given the amount of personal and sensitive data we store and transmit digitally. Here are a few of the possible outcomes of a breach:

Identity Theft: This occurs when attackers gain access to personal information, such as social security numbers and bank account information, which can be used to impersonate the victim.

Financial Loss: Cybersecurity breaches can result in significant financial loss from the theft of banking details, payment card information, or unauthorized withdrawals.

Loss of Privacy: Private and sensitive data, like medical records or personal emails, can be exposed during a data breach.

Damage to Reputation: A cybersecurity breach can also damage an individual's reputation, particularly if personal and private conversations or data are revealed.

The Importance of Personal Cybersecurity

Given the potential ramifications of a breach, it is clear that personal cybersecurity is not an area to neglect. We live in an era where we perform many of our daily activities online. From online shopping and banking to social media and remote work, our lives are increasingly intertwined with the digital world. As such, it is crucial to protect our digital identity and personal information just as vigilantly as we would protect our physical possessions. Adopting a proactive approach to cybersecurity can help prevent cyber-attacks, protect personal and financial information, and preserve our digital privacy.

In the coming chapters, we will delve into more specifics about how you can protect your digital life. From creating strong passwords and ensuring secure web browsing to protecting your personal data and understanding antivirus software, we will arm you with the tools and knowledge you need to navigate the digital world safely. After all, knowledge is the first and most essential line of defense against cyber threats.

Implementing Basic Cybersecurity Measures

While cybersecurity may seem like a complex field, there are a few basic practices everyone can adopt to significantly enhance their personal cybersecurity.

Install and update security software: Antivirus and antimalware solutions can protect your devices from a wide range of threats. Regular updates are crucial as new threats continually emerge.

Keep your operating system and applications updated: Developers routinely release updates to fix vulnerabilities that cybercriminals could exploit. Ensuring your software is up-to-date helps to keep your devices secure.

Back up your data: Regularly back up your data to an external drive or a cloud service. If your system is compromised, you will still have access to your information.

Be cautious with email attachments and links: Email is a common vector for many types of cyber threats, such as phishing and malware. Be wary of unsolicited emails and never download an attachment or click a link unless you are certain it is safe.

Emerging Trends in Cybersecurity

The field of cybersecurity is continually evolving as new technologies emerge and cyber threats become more sophisticated. Here are a few of the key trends shaping the cybersecurity landscape:

Artificial Intelligence (AI) and Machine Learning (ML) in Cybersecurity: AI and ML are increasingly being used to detect and respond to cyber threats more effectively. They can identify patterns and anomalies that might indicate a cyberattack, often more quickly than a human could.

Increased Focus on Mobile Security: As smartphones and tablets become more powerful, they are increasingly targeted by cybercriminals. There is a growing focus on developing more robust mobile security solutions.

Cloud Security: As more data is stored in the cloud, ensuring this information is secure is a top priority. Many organizations are investing in cloud security infrastructure to protect sensitive data.

Privacy Legislation: In response to rising public concern about data privacy, governments worldwide are enacting laws to protect citizens' data. Individuals and organizations need to be aware of these regulations to ensure compliance.

The Importance of Cybersecurity Education

Educating yourself about cybersecurity is one of the best defenses against cyber threats. This involves staying informed about the latest types of threats and best practices for mitigating these risks. Cybersecurity is a shared responsibility. By protecting your personal data, you are also helping to safeguard your community from cyber threats.

Becoming Cyber Resilient

Ultimately, the goal of personal cybersecurity is to become cyber resilient. Cyber resilience refers to the ability to prepare for, respond to, and recover from a cyberattack. By implementing robust cybersecurity measures and having a plan in place for responding to cyber threats, you can minimize the damage and recover more quickly if a breach occurs.

In the following chapters, we will delve deeper into these topics, giving you practical advice and strategies to enhance your cybersecurity. Whether you are an individual looking to protect your personal data or a small business owner seeking to safeguard your business, this guide will provide the tools you need to strengthen your cybersecurity and become more cyber resilient.

As we dive into more specific areas of personal cybersecurity, it is essential to remember that cybersecurity is not a one-time task but an ongoing process. The digital landscape is continually changing, with new threats emerging all the time. Regularly reviewing and updating your cybersecurity practices is key to maintaining a strong defense against these evolving threats.

In the next chapter, we will tackle one of the most crucial aspects of personal cybersecurity: creating strong, unique passwords. Poor password practices are one of the most common ways cybercriminals gain access to personal data, so mastering password security is a vital step in your cybersecurity journey.

Chapter 2: Creating Strong Passwords

When it comes to personal cybersecurity, creating strong, unique passwords is one of the most crucial steps you can take. The use of weak or duplicated passwords is one of the most common causes of security breaches. In this chapter, we will explore why it is important to use robust passwords, common password pitfalls to avoid, and how to create strong, secure passwords that are difficult for cybercriminals to crack.

The Importance of Strong Passwords

Passwords are essentially the keys to your online identity. They protect your personal, financial, and professional information from unauthorized access. However, with the increasing sophistication of cybercriminals and their tools, weak passwords can be easily cracked, leading to security breaches.

In many instances, cybercriminals use a method known as brute forcing, where they systematically check all possible passwords until the correct one is found. The simpler the password, the quicker it can be deciphered. Therefore, the more complex your password, the more secure your accounts are.

Common Password Pitfalls

Many people fall into bad habits when creating passwords. Some of the most common password pitfalls include:

Reusing Passwords: One of the most common password mistakes is using the same password across multiple accounts. If one account is breached, all accounts sharing that password are at risk.

Choosing Obvious Passwords: Using easily guessable information like "password," "123456," "qwerty," or personal information like your name, birth date, or pet's name makes it easy for cybercriminals to guess your password.

Short Passwords: Short passwords are easier to crack than longer ones. Each character you add to your password increases the time it takes for a brute force attack to succeed.

Not Changing Passwords Regularly: While it can be a hassle, constantly changing your passwords can prevent unauthorized access, especially if a service you use has been breached without your knowledge.

Creating Strong Passwords

Creating a strong password involves making it long, complex, and unique. Here is how to achieve each of these criteria:

Length: Aim for a minimum of twelve characters. The longer your password, the more secure it is. Long passwords are more challenging to crack than shorter ones because they require more guesses to break.

Complexity: Include numbers, symbols, and both uppercase and lowercase letters in your passwords. This makes them harder to guess. Avoid using obvious substitutions like "0" for "o" or "$" for "s," as these are well-known to cybercriminals.

Uniqueness: Each of your passwords should be unique. That way, if one account is compromised, your other accounts remain safe.

One effective method for creating a strong password is to think of a phrase or sentence. Take the first letter of each word, change some letters to numbers or symbols and mix up the capitalization. For example, "I love to read books on the beach!" might become "iL2RoTB!". It is both complex and memorable.

While these strategies can help create individual strong passwords, managing them can quickly become unwieldy. That is where password managers come in. They help generate and store complex passwords securely, making it easier to maintain good password hygiene without having to memorize dozens of complex passwords.

In the next part of this chapter, we will delve into password managers, how they can enhance your cybersecurity, and how to use them effectively. We will also look at multi-factor authentication, another crucial aspect of secure password management that adds an additional layer of security to your online accounts. Through the combination of strong passwords, the use of password managers, and multi-factor authentication, you can significantly enhance the security of your online accounts and protect your digital identity.

Password Managers

As we strive to create unique and complex passwords for all of our online accounts, it is not feasible to remember them all. That is where password managers come in. A password manager is a software application that stores and manages the passwords that a user has for various online accounts and security features. Password managers store the passwords in an encrypted format and provide secure access to all the password information with the help of a master password.

There are numerous password managers available, some of which are free, while others require a subscription. Notable options include LastPass, 1Password, and Dashlane. When selecting a password manager, consider factors such as its security features, ease of use, cost, and whether it offers a multi-platform solution that can be used across your devices.

Using Password Managers Effectively

Password managers are not just about storing your passwords; they can also help you create strong, unique passwords for each of your accounts. Here is how to get the most out of a password manager:

Use a strong master password: Your master password is the key to your password manager. It needs to be strong and unique. It is also the one password you will need to remember, so ensure it is memorable.

Take advantage of password generation: Most password managers offer a password generation feature. Use it to create complex passwords for each of your accounts.

Keep your password manager updated: Software updates often include patches for security vulnerabilities. Regular updates can keep your password manager as secure as possible.

Multi-factor Authentication

Multi-factor authentication (MFA) adds an extra layer of security to your accounts. Even if someone manages to obtain your password, they will be unable to access your account without passing the second layer of authentication.

MFA can involve something you know (like a password or PIN), something you have (like a smartphone or a hardware token), or something you are (like a fingerprint or other biometric factor). One of the most common forms of MFA is a temporary code sent to your smartphone or generated by an authenticator app.

Implementing Multi-factor Authentication

To implement multi-factor authentication, follow these steps:

Check if the service supports MFA: Many online services offer MFA, but it is often not enabled by default. Check your account settings or the service's security settings to see if it is available.

Choose your second factor: If MFA is available, you will often have several options for your second factor. Choose the one that suits you best. A common choice is receiving a code via SMS, but using an authenticator app is often more secure.

Set up a backup method: It is a good idea to set up a backup method in case you cannot access your primary second factor. This could be a backup phone number or one-time use backup codes.

Test your MFA: Once you've set up MFA, sign out of the account and sign back in to make sure everything is working correctly.

Using strong, unique passwords, taking advantage of password managers, and enabling multi-factor authentication are all essential practices for maintaining your personal cybersecurity. In the next chapter, we will move from your accounts' passwords to your web browsing habits. Safe and secure browsing is another critical element of personal cybersecurity, helping to prevent cyber-attacks and keep your private data secure.

Cybersecurity is an ongoing process, with each step contributing to a stronger overall defense against cyber threats. With the foundation of strong password practices, you are well on your way to safeguarding your digital life.

Chapter 3: Secure Web Browsing

While strong passwords and multi-factor authentication are crucial for protecting your individual accounts, the way you navigate the web also significantly impacts your personal cybersecurity. Every time you go online, there are potential risks, from websites loaded with malware to Wi-Fi networks primed for eavesdropping. This chapter will explore strategies and best practices for secure web browsing, helping you minimize the risk of cyber threats.

Understanding the Risks

Internet browsing may seem harmless, but various threats can lurk beneath the surface. Here are some of the risks associated with web browsing:

Malware: Some websites contain malicious software, or malware, which can be downloaded and installed on your device without your knowledge. This can lead to data theft, computer damage, and other security problems.

Phishing: Deceptive websites may attempt to trick you into providing personal or financial information. These sites often mimic legitimate websites, like your bank or email service.

Unsecured Networks: Browsing the internet on unsecured Wi-Fi networks can expose your data to interception. Cybercriminals can 'listen in' to these networks and potentially capture the information you send and receive.

Data Breaches: If a website you use suffers a data breach, your personal information may be exposed. This could include your name, email address, and even your password.

HTTPS and SSL/TLS

When you are browsing the web, one of the first things to look for is whether a website is secure. Secure websites use HTTPS (Hypertext Transfer Protocol Secure) instead of HTTP. The 'S' in HTTPS indicates that the website is using SSL (Secure Sockets Layer) or TLS (Transport Layer Security) encryption protocols to secure the connection between your device and the website.

This encryption ensures that any data you send to the website (such as credit card information when you are shopping online) cannot be read by anyone else. You can tell if a website uses HTTPS by looking at the URL in your browser's address bar. If it starts with 'https://', the site is secure. Some browsers also display a padlock icon to indicate a secure connection.

Keeping Your Browser Updated

Your web browser is one of your primary gateways to the internet, and keeping it updated is crucial for secure browsing. Browser developers regularly release updates that patch security vulnerabilities and add new security features. Failing to update your browser can leave you exposed to threats that have been fixed in more recent versions.

Most modern browsers update automatically by default, but it is good to manually check for updates occasionally to make sure you are up-to-date. You can usually do this in the browser's settings menu.

Using Private Browsing Modes

Most web browsers offer a private browsing mode (also known as incognito mode). When you browse in private mode, the browser does not save your browsing history, cookies, or form data. This can be useful if you are using a public computer and do not want to leave any personal information behind.

However, private browsing modes do not make you anonymous on the internet, and they do not protect your data from being intercepted by others on the network. For that, you need tools like VPNs and secure Wi-Fi networks, which we will discuss in the next part of this chapter. We will also delve into the importance of firewalls and ad blockers, as well as safe practices for downloading and installing software from the internet. Secure web browsing is a multifaceted endeavor, but with the right tools and knowledge, you can significantly reduce your exposure to cyber threats.

Virtual Private Networks (VPNs)

A Virtual Private Network, or VPN, is a tool that creates a private network from a public internet connection, offering a valuable layer of security and privacy. VPNs mask your IP address, making your online actions virtually untraceable. More importantly, they establish secure and encrypted connections, providing greater privacy than even a secured Wi-Fi hotspot.

VPNs are especially important if you frequently use public Wi-Fi networks, which are typically not very secure. By routing your connection through a VPN, you can ensure that any data you send or receive is encrypted and safe from prying eyes.

Firewalls

A firewall is another critical tool for secure web browsing. Essentially, a firewall is a barrier or shield that prevents unauthorized access to or from a private network. Firewalls monitor and control incoming and outgoing network traffic based on predetermined security rules. They establish a barrier between a trusted internal network and an untrusted external network, such as the internet.

Firewalls can be hardware or software. Most modern operating systems come with built-in firewalls, which are typically turned on by default. Be sure to check your firewall settings to ensure that it is active and configured correctly.

Ad Blockers

Ad blockers are browser extensions that prevent advertisements from being displayed on websites. While ads can be annoying, ad blockers play a more important role in cybersecurity: they prevent ad-based malware (malvertising) from infecting your device.

Malvertising involves injecting malicious code into legitimate online advertising networks. The code can be used to track your activities or, worse, redirect you to sites that download malware onto your device. By using an ad blocker, you can protect yourself from these threats.

Safe Downloading and Installing

Finally, be cautious when downloading and installing software or other files from the internet. Cybercriminals often disguise malware as legitimate software to trick users into installing it.

Here are some tips for safe downloading and installing:

Use reputable sites: Only download software from trusted sources. If you are unsure about a website, do some research to see if it is reliable.

Look for HTTPS: Only download files from websites that use HTTPS. This indicates that the connection between your device and the website is secure.

Check reviews and ratings: If you are downloading an app from an app store, check its reviews and ratings. Apps with poor reviews or low ratings might be malicious.

Watch for signs of malware: Be wary of files that are significantly larger or smaller than they should be, as this could indicate the presence of malware. Similarly, if a file has an unexpected format (like a .exe file when you were expecting a .doc file), it might be dangerous.

By incorporating these strategies into your web browsing habits, you can greatly enhance your personal cybersecurity. However, remember that technology is only one piece of the puzzle. It is equally important to develop a security-minded attitude. Be cautious, be vigilant, and remember that if something seems too good to be true, it probably is. In the next chapter, we will explore another essential aspect of personal cybersecurity: social media and online privacy. Stay tuned, and stay secure!

Chapter 4: Email Security

Email is a crucial part of daily life, serving as our primary communication tool for work, personal relationships, and online services. However, it is also a common vector for cyberattacks. This chapter will discuss the steps you can take to secure your email, protect your personal information, and reduce your risk of falling victim to cyber threats.

Understanding the Threats

Knowing the types of email threats is the first step towards securing your email. Some of the most common threats include:

Phishing: Phishing emails attempt to trick you into revealing personal information, such as your passwords or credit card numbers. These emails often mimic legitimate organizations and contain links to fake websites where your information is collected.

Malware: Some emails contain malicious attachments or links to sites that download malware onto your device. This malware can damage your computer, steal personal information, or even give a cybercriminal control over your device.

Spam: While spam is often merely annoying rather than harmful, some spam emails contain malicious links, scams, or phishing attempts.

Spoofing: Email spoofing is when a sender masquerades as someone else by falsifying the email header information. It is a tactic often used in phishing and spam campaigns.

Securing Your Email Account

Your first line of defense in email security is securing your email account itself. This involves strong password practices, which we discussed in

Chapter 2, and using two-factor authentication (2FA), which adds an extra layer of security to your account.

Many email providers offer 2FA. Once it is set up, you will be required to enter a second form of verification (usually a code sent to your mobile device) in addition to your password when logging in. This makes it much more difficult for an unauthorized person to access your account, even if they have your password.

Recognizing and Handling Suspicious Emails

The next step in email security is learning how to recognize and handle suspicious emails. Here are some tips:

Check the sender's email address: Phishing emails often come from addresses that resemble legitimate ones, but with slight alterations. If the email supposedly comes from a service you use but the email address does not match the one on the official website, it is probably a phishing attempt.

Look for poor grammar and spelling: Many phishing emails originate from non-English-speaking countries and contain poor grammar and spelling. Professional organizations usually have teams that ensure their emails are grammatically correct and free of spelling errors.

Be wary of urgent or threatening language: Phishing emails often use urgent or threatening language to scare you into acting without thinking. They might say your account has been compromised and you need to enter your password to confirm your identity, or that you owe money and need to pay immediately.

Do not click on suspicious links or download attachments: If you are unsure about an email, do not click on any links or download any attachments it contains. They might lead to malicious websites or contain malware.

In the second half of this chapter, we will dive deeper into the steps you can take to secure your email. We will discuss strategies like email encryption, the importance of keeping your contacts informed if you are compromised, how to handle spam, and what to do if you suspect you have fallen victim to an email scam. Just like with secure web browsing, secure email practices require a mix of the right tools and a vigilant mindset. Stay tuned to enhance your email security and safeguard your online communication.

Email Encryption

Encrypting your email adds an additional layer of security by encoding your messages so only the intended recipient can read them. While many email providers use TLS (Transport Layer Security) to encrypt emails in transit, end-to-end encryption – like that offered by PGP (Pretty Good Privacy) or S/MIME (Secure/Multipurpose Internet Mail Extensions) – ensures that your emails are encrypted from the moment they are sent to the moment they are opened.

Using email encryption can be a bit complex, especially when first starting out. However, there are many resources available online to guide you through the process, and some email services even offer built-in end-to-end encryption options.

Keeping Your Contacts Informed

In the unfortunate event that your email is compromised, it is important to let your contacts know as soon as possible. This is because attackers often use compromised accounts to send phishing emails, spam, or malware to the contacts listed in the account. By informing your contacts, you can help protect them from falling victim to these attacks.

To do this, you might need to use an alternative communication method, like phone calls, text messages, or a secondary email account. Explain the situation, advise them not to open any suspicious emails that appear to be from you, and let them know you are working to resolve the issue.

Handling Spam

While spam can be annoying, there are several steps you can take to manage it effectively:

Do not reply to spam: Replying can confirm to the spammer that your email address is active, leading to more spam.

Use a spam filter: Most email services have a built-in spam filter that automatically identifies and moves spam emails to a separate folder.

Report spam: Reporting spam helps your email service improve its spam filters. Look for the 'Report spam' or similar button in your email interface.

Be careful with your email address: The more people who have your email address, the more likely it is to end up on a spam list. Only give out your email address when necessary, and consider using a secondary email address for non-essential services.

What to Do If You're Scammed

If you suspect you have fallen for an email scam, take the following steps:

Change your passwords: Start with your email password, then change the passwords for any accounts linked to your email, especially if they contain sensitive information.

Contact your bank: If the scam involved financial information, contact your bank immediately. They can monitor your accounts for fraudulent activity and possibly reverse any illicit transactions.

Report the scam: Reporting the scam can help authorities track down the culprits and prevent others from falling victim. In the U.S., you can report email scams to the Federal Trade Commission (FTC) through their website.

Check your computer for malware: If you clicked on any links or downloaded any files from the scam email, your device might be infected with malware. Run a scan with a reputable security software to identify and remove any threats.

Securing your email is a vital part of your overall cybersecurity strategy. By understanding the threats, using the right tools, and staying vigilant, you can significantly reduce your risk of falling victim to email scams and attacks. In the next chapter, we will delve into social media and online privacy, further exploring how to protect your information and maintain a secure presence online.

Chapter 5: Social Media Safety

Social media platforms are wonderful tools for staying connected with friends, family, and the world at large. However, they also present unique cybersecurity challenges. This chapter will explore strategies for using social media safely, including setting strong privacy settings, avoiding phishing attempts, and being cautious with the information you share.

Understanding the Threats

Just like with email and web browsing, the first step towards safe social media usage is understanding the associated threats. These can include:

Phishing and Scams: Phishers often use social media to trick people into revealing personal information. They might send messages pretending to be a friend in need, a lottery or sweepstakes "winner", or a reputable company requesting a password reset.

Identity Theft: Cybercriminals can use the information you share on social media to steal your identity. They might piece together information from various posts to answer your security questions, or create fake accounts in your name to defraud others.

Harassment and Stalking: Some people use social media to harass or stalk others. They might send threatening messages, post abusive comments, or use the information you have shared to track your activities.

Data Breaches: If a social media platform suffers a data breach, your personal information could be exposed. This could include everything from your email address and password to private messages and photos.

Securing Your Account

As with your email account, the first line of defense for your social media accounts is a strong password and, where available, two-factor authentication (2FA). We have covered these topics in detail in previous chapters, but it is worth repeating their importance. Using a unique, complex password for each of your social media accounts and enabling 2FA where possible can significantly reduce the risk of unauthorized access.

Privacy Settings

Social media platforms typically offer a range of privacy settings that allow you to control who can see your posts, send you messages, see your list of friends, and more. Spend some time exploring these settings for each platform you use. You might choose to make your account entirely private, allowing only approved friends to see your posts, or you might simply limit certain information, like your list of friends or your email address.

Keep in mind that default privacy settings often lean towards openness to encourage more interaction. If you have not checked your privacy settings before, you might be sharing more information than you realize.

Be Cautious With Friend Requests

While it can be exciting to receive new friend requests, be cautious about who you accept. Fake accounts are common on social media, and cybercriminals can use them to access your information or send you phishing links.

Before accepting a friend request, look at the person's profile. Do they have a lot of friends, or just a few? Do they have posts dating back over time, or is their account brand new? If anything looks suspicious, it is best to reject the request.

In the second half of this chapter, we will delve deeper into the do's and don'ts of social media posting, how to recognize and avoid social media scams, and what to do if your social media account is compromised. With a mindful approach and a firm grasp on your privacy settings, you can enjoy social media while still maintaining a strong level of cybersecurity.

Think Before You Post

Before you post anything on social media, consider the potential implications. Could the information be used to answer a security question (like "What's your mother's maiden name?" or "What was the name of your first pet?")? Could it give a cybercriminal information they could use to scam you or a friend? Could it let a potential burglar know that your house will be empty?

As a rule, avoid posting sensitive personal information like your home address, phone number, or financial information. Also, be cautious about posting information that could be used in social engineering attacks – for instance, if you post about losing your wallet, a scammer might see it and send you a message pretending to be from your bank.

Recognizing and Avoiding Social Media Scams

Just as with email, phishing scams are common on social media. These might come in the form of messages, comments, or posts that try to trick you into revealing personal information, clicking on a malicious link, or downloading malware.

Be skeptical of any unsolicited messages that ask for personal information, even if they appear to come from a friend. If you receive a message like this, contact your friend through another method to confirm that they sent it.

Also, be wary of posts that promise incredible deals or giveaways. If something seems too good to be true, it probably is.

Regularly Review Your Privacy Settings and Friends List

Social media platforms frequently update their policies and settings, which can sometimes result in changes to your privacy settings. To ensure your settings are still configured as you want them, make a habit of reviewing them regularly.

Similarly, it is a good idea to review your friends list periodically. If you notice any friends that you do not recognize, it could be a sign that you have accepted a friend request from a scam account. Removing these "friends" can help protect your information.

What to Do If Your Social Media Account Is Compromised

If you suspect that your social media account has been compromised, take the following steps:

Change your password: This should be your first step. If the attacker has changed your password and you cannot access your account, contact the social media platform's support team immediately.

Check your settings: If you can access your account, check your settings to see if anything has been changed. Look at your privacy settings, email address, linked accounts, and so on.

Scan your device for malware: If your account were compromised, it could be because your device is infected with malware. Run a scan with a reputable security software to identify and remove any threats.

Inform your contacts: Just like with email, let your friends know that your account was compromised to prevent them from falling victim to any scams sent from your account.

Social media is a fantastic tool, but it can also expose you to cybersecurity threats. By following these guidelines, you can enjoy the benefits of social media while minimizing the risks. Remember, cybersecurity is not a one-time thing – it requires ongoing vigilance. Keep learning, stay alert, and continue to prioritize your digital safety. In our next chapter, we will explore mobile device security, another crucial aspect of personal cybersecurity in today's digital world.

Chapter 6: Mobile Device Security

Mobile devices such as smartphones and tablets have become essential tools for communication, work, and entertainment. They store a vast amount of personal data, making them attractive targets for cybercriminals. In this chapter, we will explore the steps you can take to secure your mobile devices and protect your personal information.

Understanding the Threats

To secure your mobile device, you need to understand the threats. Here are some of the most common:

Malware: Mobile devices can be infected with malware, just like computers. This can happen through downloading malicious apps, clicking on malicious links in emails or text messages, or visiting malicious websites.

Unsecured Networks: Using public Wi-Fi networks can expose your device to risks. Cybercriminals may intercept your data on unsecured networks, gaining access to your personal information, login credentials, and more.

Physical Theft: Mobile devices are compact and portable, making them prone to loss or theft. If your device falls into the wrong hands, all the data stored on it is at risk.

App Permissions: Some apps request permissions that invade your privacy or expose your data. For instance, a simple game might ask for access to your contacts, call logs, or location, even though it does not need this information to function.

Securing Your Mobile Device

Securing your mobile device involves several steps, starting with the device's physical security.

Lock Your Device: Use a strong passcode, pattern, or biometric authentication like fingerprint recognition or facial recognition to lock your device. This can prevent unauthorized access if your device is lost or stolen.

Keep Your Device with You: To prevent physical theft or loss, always keep your device with you or in a secure location. Never leave it unattended in public places.

Remote Wipe: Set up a feature to erase your device's data remotely in case it is lost or stolen. Both iOS and Android offer this feature, which can protect your data if your device falls into the wrong hands.

Keeping Your Device Updated

Regular software updates are crucial for mobile device security. These updates often include patches for security vulnerabilities that have been discovered since the last version of the software. Keeping your device updated can protect you from threats targeting these vulnerabilities.

Regularly Check for Updates: Make a habit of checking for and installing updates to both your device's operating system and the apps you use.

Enable Automatic Updates: Consider enabling automatic updates, if available. This ensures that your device stays updated even if you forget to check for updates.

Download Apps Wisely

The apps you download can significantly impact your mobile device's security.

Download from Trusted Sources: Only download apps from trusted sources like the Apple App Store for iOS devices and Google Play Store for

Android devices. These platforms have security measures in place to reduce the risk of malicious apps.

Check App Reviews and Permissions: Before downloading an app, check its reviews and ratings, and read the list of permissions it requests. If an app asks for permissions that do not make sense (like a flashlight app requesting access to your contacts), it is a red flag.

In the second half of this chapter, we will discuss more in-depth security measures, such as secure network practices, data encryption, safe browsing habits, and security apps. By taking these steps to secure your mobile device, you can keep your personal information safe and enjoy your device with peace of mind.

Secure Network Practices

While it is convenient to connect to the internet wherever you are, be mindful of the networks you join with your mobile device.

Avoid Public Wi-Fi When Possible: Public Wi-Fi networks are often unsecured, meaning data transmitted over them can be intercepted. Avoid using public Wi-Fi for activities that involve sensitive data, such as online banking or shopping.

Use a VPN: A Virtual Private Network (VPN) encrypts your internet connection, making it much harder for anyone to intercept your data. Consider using a VPN whenever you connect to a public Wi-Fi network.

Encrypt Your Data

Data encryption converts your data into a code that can only be accessed with the correct encryption key, offering an additional layer of security.

Enable Encryption on Your Device: Both iOS and Android devices come with an option to encrypt your data. Look for this option in your security settings.

Encrypt Your SD Card: If your device has an SD card, consider encrypting it as well. This can prevent someone from removing the card and accessing your data on another device.

Safe Browsing Habits

Just as with computers, safe browsing habits are essential on mobile devices.

Beware of Phishing Attempts: Phishing websites and emails can be just as dangerous on mobile devices as they are on computers. Be cautious of any unexpected links, even if they appear to be from a trustworthy source.

Update Your Browser: Just like your device's operating system and apps, keep your browser updated. Updates often include security patches that can protect you from threats.

Use a Secure Browser: Consider using a browser that prioritizes security and privacy. These browsers often include features like tracking protection, ad blocking, and data encryption.

Security Apps

Several apps can enhance your mobile device's security.

Antivirus App: Just as with a computer, an antivirus app can help protect your mobile device from malware. Look for a reputable app with high ratings and positive reviews.

App Lockers: These apps can add an extra layer of security to your device by requiring a passcode, pattern, or fingerprint to open specific apps.

VPN Apps: A VPN app can encrypt your internet connection, making it harder for anyone to intercept your data.

Backup Your Data

Regularly backing up your data ensures that you will not lose everything if your device is lost, stolen, or compromised.

Use Cloud Backup Services: Both iOS and Android offer cloud backup services that can automatically back up your data. These services can back up a range of data, including contacts, photos, and app data.

Regularly Check Your Backup: It is a good practice to check your backup regularly to ensure that it is working correctly and backing up the right data.

By following the practices outlined in this chapter, you can significantly enhance the security of your mobile devices. Remember, the goal of cybersecurity is not to eliminate all risks – that is nearly impossible – but to minimize risks and know how to respond if something does go wrong. In our next chapter, we will examine online shopping and banking, areas of digital life that require particular attention to security due to the sensitive nature of the data involved.

Chapter 7: Protecting Personal Data

Protecting your personal data is a crucial aspect of maintaining your overall cybersecurity. Personal data refers to any data that could be used to identify you, including your name, address, social security number, financial information, and more. In the wrong hands, this information could be used for identity theft, fraud, and other malicious activities. This chapter will discuss ways to protect your personal data online.

Understanding the Threats

The first step towards protecting your personal data is understanding the potential threats:

Data Breaches: When a company's database is hacked, your personal data stored within their systems could be exposed.

Phishing Attempts: Phishing is an attempt by cybercriminals to trick you into providing personal information by pretending to be a legitimate organization.

Unsecured Websites: If a website is not secure (i.e., it does not use HTTPS), any data you submit can potentially be intercepted by cybercriminals.

Public Wi-Fi Networks: When using a public Wi-Fi network, your data can be intercepted by anyone else on the network.

Creating Layers of Protection

Protecting your personal data involves creating layers of security. This way, if one layer is breached, others still stand.

Use Strong, Unique Passwords: As discussed in Chapter 2, strong, unique passwords can protect your online accounts from unauthorized access.

Never use the same password for multiple accounts.

Enable Two-Factor Authentication (2FA): 2FA provides an additional layer of security by requiring two types of identification before granting access to an account. This often involves a password and a temporary code sent to your mobile device.

Secure Your Devices: Make sure that your devices are secured with a strong password or biometric authentication, and keep your devices' software up-to-date. Remember to install reputable security software, as discussed in Chapter 6.

Be Cautious When Sharing Personal Data

Be wary about who you share your personal data with and under what circumstances.

Only Share What's Necessary: Some websites ask for more personal data than they need. If you are not comfortable with the amount of data a site is asking for, do not be afraid to ask why it is necessary.

Use Fake Answers for Security Questions: When setting up security questions, consider using answers that are not easily discoverable. Cybercriminals could potentially find real answers by searching your social media profiles or public records.

Maintain Privacy on Social Networks

Social networks can be a goldmine of personal data for cybercriminals.

Check Your Privacy Settings: Review your privacy settings regularly and limit who can see your posts, your list of friends, and the information in your profile.

Be Careful About What You Post: Be cautious about posting personal data that could be used to answer security questions or that might be of interest to cybercriminals, such as your home address or when your home will be empty.

In the second half of this chapter, we will discuss how to handle your personal data in financial transactions, as well as the steps you can take if your personal data is compromised. By following these guidelines, you can significantly reduce the risk of your personal data falling into the wrong hands.

Financial Transactions and Personal Data

When shopping or banking online, protecting your personal data becomes especially important due to the sensitive nature of the transactions.

Shop from Secure Websites Only: Always check whether the site uses HTTPS before entering any personal or financial data. The 'S' in HTTPS stands for secure, indicating that the data you enter is being encrypted.

Use a Credit Card or Secure Payment Service: Credit cards often come with fraud protection features that debit cards do not. Alternatively, consider using a secure payment service like PayPal, which keeps your credit card number hidden from the seller.

Beware of Phishing Attempts: As discussed earlier, phishing attempts are a common tactic used by cybercriminals to gather personal information. Be cautious of emails or messages that ask for personal or financial information, even if they appear to come from a trusted source.

Regularly Monitor Your Accounts

Regularly checking your accounts can help you detect any suspicious activity early.

Regularly Check Your Bank and Credit Card Statements: Look for any transactions that you do not recognize. If you find any, report them to your bank immediately.

Review Your Online Accounts: Regularly check your online accounts (like your email or social media accounts) for any changes that you did not make.

What to Do If Your Personal Data is Compromised

Despite your best efforts, there may be times when your personal data is compromised. Here is what to do if that happens:

Change Your Passwords: If you suspect that an account has been compromised, change its password immediately. If you were using the same password for multiple accounts, change those as well.

Contact Your Bank: If your financial data has been compromised, contact your bank immediately. They can help you protect your accounts and guide you on the next steps.

Report Identity Theft: If you suspect that your personal data has been used to commit fraud or other crimes, report it to your local law enforcement and your country's relevant authorities.

Monitor Your Accounts More Closely: After a data breach, be extra vigilant in monitoring your accounts for any suspicious activity.

Consider a Credit Freeze: If your social security number or other critical personal data has been compromised, consider freezing your credit to prevent cybercriminals from opening new accounts in your name.

By taking these steps, you can minimize the damage and recover more quickly from a data breach.

Conclusion

Protecting your personal data is an ongoing process. As technology evolves, new threats will emerge, and you will need to adapt your security practices accordingly. Stay informed about the latest cybersecurity threats and solutions, and do not underestimate the importance of protecting your personal data. Remember, cybersecurity is not a destination, but a journey that requires constant vigilance and learning.

In the next chapter, we will dive into the topic of online scams, their different types, and effective ways to spot and avoid them. This knowledge is crucial, as scams often serve as the entry point for numerous cybersecurity threats.

Chapter 8: Safe Online Shopping

The advent of online shopping has made it incredibly easy to purchase almost anything without leaving your home. However, it is crucial to ensure your personal and financial information is secure during these transactions. This chapter will guide you through the practices for maintaining safety while shopping online.

Understanding the Risks

Before we dive into the best practices, it is essential to understand the potential risks involved in online shopping:

Data Breaches: Online retailers store your personal and financial information. If their security systems are compromised, your data could be stolen.

Fraudulent Websites: Some websites pose as legitimate online stores but are actually set up to collect your personal and financial information.

Phishing Attempts: You may receive emails that look like they are from legitimate retailers but are actually attempts to steal your information.

Unsecured Websites: Not all websites use secure protocols (HTTPS), which means the data you transmit might not be encrypted and could be intercepted.

Safe Online Shopping Practices

Implementing the following practices can significantly improve your online shopping security:

Shop from Reputable Retailers

Stick with well-known retailers that you are familiar with. If you are considering buying from a company you have not heard of before, do some research. Look for reviews or complaints about the company online.

Look for HTTPS

Before entering any personal or financial information, make sure the website uses HTTPS. This means the data you submit is encrypted and much harder for cybercriminals to intercept. You can see if a website uses HTTPS by looking for a padlock icon to the left of the web address in your browser.

Do not Shop on Public Wi-Fi

As convenient as it may be, avoid shopping online when connected to a public Wi-Fi network. These networks are often unsecured, meaning the data you transmit could be intercepted by others on the network.

Secure Your Devices

Ensure your devices are secure by using strong, unique passwords, keeping your operating system and apps updated, and installing reputable security software. A compromised device can lead to compromised data.

Use Strong, Unique Passwords for Online Accounts

As we have mentioned in previous chapters, using strong, unique passwords for each of your online accounts is crucial. If a cybercriminal manages to crack your password for one account, they will not be able to access your other accounts.

Consider Using a Credit Card or Secure Payment Service

Credit cards often have better fraud protection than debit cards. If a cybercriminal does manage to steal your credit card information, you can report the fraudulent charges and not have to pay for them. Alternatively, you can use secure payment services like PayPal, which keep your credit card information hidden from the seller.

In the second half of this chapter, we will cover additional protective measures, like two-factor authentication, monitoring bank statements, using private browsing, and being wary of too-good-to-be-true deals. By following these guidelines, you can shop online with peace of mind, knowing that you are doing your part to protect your personal and financial information.

Enabling Two-Factor Authentication

Two-factor authentication (2FA) provides an additional layer of security for your online accounts. When 2FA is enabled, you will need to provide two forms of identification to access your account - usually your password and a temporary code sent to your phone or email. This means that even if a cybercriminal manages to crack your password, they will not be able to access your account without the temporary code.

Monitoring Your Bank Statements

Regularly check your bank statements for any transactions that you do not recognize. If you notice anything suspicious, report it to your bank immediately. Many banks have a zero-liability policy for fraudulent charges, but you usually need to report them within a certain timeframe.

Using Private Browsing

Consider using your browser's private browsing mode when shopping online. This can help protect your privacy by preventing the websites you visit from collecting your browsing data.

Being Wary of Too-Good-to-Be-True Deals

If a deal seems too good to be true, it probably is. Be especially cautious of emails or websites offering extremely low prices. They might be scams set up to steal your information or sell you counterfeit goods.

Avoid Clicking on Email Links

Avoid clicking on links in emails, especially if the email seems suspicious. These links could lead to fraudulent websites or download malware onto your device. Instead, type the retailer's web address directly into your browser.

Updating Your Devices and Applications

Ensure your devices and all your applications are up-to-date. Updates often include security patches that protect against new threats. This includes your browser and any apps you use to shop online.

Conclusion

Shopping online is convenient and often allows you to find better deals than you might in physical stores. However, it is essential to take steps to protect your personal and financial information. By following the practices outlined in this chapter, you can significantly enhance your online shopping security.

In the next chapter, we will delve into online banking security, another essential aspect of personal cybersecurity. Similar to online shopping, online banking also involves transactions of sensitive information. However, it comes with its unique set of challenges and requires specific protective measures.

CHAPTER 9: UNDERSTANDING AND USING ANTIVIRUS SOFTWARE

As you navigate the digital world, your device collects all sorts of files and data from different sources. This data could include potentially harmful software like viruses, spyware, and other types of malware. Antivirus software plays a crucial role in protecting your devices and your personal information from these threats. In this chapter, we will explore what antivirus software is, why it is essential, and how to use it effectively.

What is Antivirus Software?

Antivirus software is a program designed to prevent, search for, detect, and remove software viruses and other malicious software. These programs are an essential part of a broader cybersecurity strategy because they provide a line of defense against various forms of malware that can compromise your devices or data.

How Does Antivirus Software Work?

Antivirus software operates on two primary mechanisms: signature-based detection and behavior-based detection.

Signature-Based Detection: Every piece of malware has a unique code or 'signature'. Antivirus software maintains a vast database of known malware signatures. The software continuously scans your computer for files containing these signatures. When it finds a match, it isolates or deletes the offending file.

Behavior-Based Detection: This method involves identifying malware based on its behavior. If a program or file is acting suspiciously (e.g., trying to access protected files or modify system settings), the antivirus software flags it as potentially malicious.

Importance of Antivirus Software

Protecting Your Devices: Viruses and malware can slow down your devices, cause them to crash, or make them unusable. By preventing malware infections, antivirus software helps keep your devices running smoothly.

Preventing Identity Theft: Many forms of malware are designed to steal personal information. Antivirus software helps protect your personal data and prevents identity theft.

Protecting Your Network: If one device on your network becomes infected with malware, the infection can quickly spread to other devices. Antivirus software helps protect your entire network.

Choosing Antivirus Software

Choosing the right antivirus software is critical. Here are a few factors to consider:

Comprehensive Protection: Choose software that offers comprehensive protection against a wide range of malware, including viruses, worms, Trojans, ransomware, spyware, and adware.

Ease of Use: The software should be user-friendly and easy to navigate. It should also provide automatic updates to stay current with the latest threats.

Performance Impact: All antivirus software will use some of your device's resources, but it should not significantly impact your device's performance.

Compatibility: The software must be compatible with your operating system and other software.

Customer Support: Choose a software provider with good customer support to help resolve any issues you may encounter.

In the second half of this chapter, we will discuss the effective use of antivirus software, how to keep it updated, run scans, interpret results, and manage quarantined files. Antivirus software, when understood and used correctly, forms a significant pillar of your personal cybersecurity strategy.

Installing and Updating Antivirus Software

Once you have chosen your antivirus software, the next step is to install it. Follow the provider's instructions to do this. After installation, you will need to ensure that your software is always up-to-date. Antivirus software relies on its database of virus signatures to identify threats, and new viruses are created every day. Therefore, it is crucial to keep your software updated to protect against the latest threats.

Regular Scans

After installation, schedule regular scans of your device. Most antivirus software allows you to schedule scans at set intervals, such as weekly or daily. Regular scans will ensure that any threats are quickly identified and dealt with. You should also run a scan if you notice your device acting unusually or if you have visited a suspicious website or downloaded a suspicious file.

Understanding Scan Results and Managing Threats

Once the antivirus software has completed a scan, it will present you with the results. The results will typically show you any threats that were found and what actions were taken. Here is how to interpret the results:

Clean/No Threats Found: This is the ideal result. It means your device appears to be free from known threats.

Threats Detected and Removed/Quarantined: If your antivirus software found threats, it would typically try to remove or quarantine them. Removed threats have been deleted from your device. Quarantined threats have been moved to a secure area of your device where they cannot do any harm.

Threats Detected but Not Removed/Quarantined: Sometimes, the antivirus software might not be able to remove or quarantine a threat. This could be because the threat is embedded in a file that the software does not have permission to modify. In such cases, you will need to follow the software's instructions to remove the threat manually.

Real-Time Protection

In addition to regular scans, most antivirus software also provides real-time protection. This means that it is constantly running in the background, scanning files as they are opened or downloaded and monitoring for suspicious behavior. Ensure that this feature is enabled to provide ongoing protection for your device.

Regular Software Updates

Just as it is important to keep your antivirus software updated, it is equally important to keep all your other software updated. Software updates often include security patches that fix vulnerabilities that viruses and other malware could exploit.

Conclusion

While antivirus software is an essential part of any cybersecurity strategy, it is not a silver bullet. It is just one part of a comprehensive approach to cybersecurity that should also include safe online habits, use of strong, unique passwords, two-factor authentication, secure browsing practices, and regular data backups.

Remember, cybersecurity is a continuous journey, not a destination. The threats are continually evolving, and so too must your defense strategies. In the next and final chapter, we will delve into the topic of keeping your digital footprint minimal and managing your online presence. By being cautious and mindful of your actions and data online, you can significantly improve your overall personal cybersecurity.

Chapter 10: Creating a Cybersecurity Plan

After understanding the importance of cybersecurity and the various practices that can enhance your safety online, it is time to develop a personal cybersecurity plan. A cybersecurity plan outlines how you will protect your digital information and what steps you will take in case of a security incident. In this chapter, we will guide you through creating a personalized plan that aligns with your digital lifestyle.

1. Assessing Your Digital Lifestyle

Everyone's digital life is unique. Some people might do online banking, shopping, and communication extensively, while others might limit their digital interactions. Understanding your digital lifestyle is crucial to knowing what kind of protection you need.

Ask yourself these questions:

What types of devices do you use? (computers, smartphones, tablets, smart home devices, etc.)

What activities do you do online? (shopping, banking, social networking, work, etc.)

What types of sensitive information might be at risk? (personal data, financial data, work data, etc.)

2. Identifying Potential Threats

Once you have an understanding of your digital lifestyle, identify the threats that could potentially harm you. For example, if you frequently shop online, you might be at risk of data breaches from retailers or fraudulent transactions. If you often use social media, you might be targeted with phishing attempts or social engineering.

3. Setting Security Goals

With a clear understanding of your digital lifestyle and potential threats, you can set security goals. These goals should address the threats you have identified and provide a clear direction for your cybersecurity plan. Your goals might include things like:

Protecting your personal information from identity theft.

Keeping your devices free from malware.

Preventing unauthorized access to your online accounts.

4. Choosing Tools and Practices

Next, decide on the tools and practices you will use to achieve your security goals. This includes everything from the security settings on your devices and online accounts to the cybersecurity software you use. Here are some factors to consider:

Password Management: As outlined in Chapter 2, strong, unique passwords are critical. A password manager can help manage your passwords effectively.

Software Updates: Keeping software up-to-date is a straightforward yet crucial practice for maintaining security.

Antivirus Software: As discussed in Chapter 9, antivirus software is a critical tool for protecting your devices from malware.

Secure Browsing Practices: As covered in Chapter 3, these practices can help protect you from threats like phishing and malware.

Data Backup: Regularly backing up your data can help you recover if you fall victim to threats like ransomware or hardware failure.

In the second half of this chapter, we will guide you through creating your cybersecurity plan, implementing it, and evaluating its effectiveness regularly. Remember, a robust cybersecurity plan is dynamic and should be updated as your digital lifestyle and the cybersecurity landscape evolve.

5. Crafting Your Cybersecurity Plan

With the assessment, goals, and tools/practices in mind, you can now craft your personal cybersecurity plan. This plan should include:

The Actions: List the specific steps you will take to achieve each of your security goals. For instance, you might decide to use a password manager to help create and store complex passwords or regularly update your antivirus software to protect against the latest threats.

The Schedule: Specify when and how often you will perform each action. Some actions need to be performed regularly, like scanning your devices for malware, while others, like setting up two-factor authentication for your online accounts, might be one-time actions.

The Metrics: Define how you will measure the success of your plan. This might involve checking that you have completed all scheduled actions or periodically testing your security to ensure it is up to scratch.

6. Implementing Your Plan

With your cybersecurity plan in place, the next step is to implement it. Start with the actions that offer the most immediate protection, such as enabling two-factor authentication on your accounts, installing antivirus software, and updating your devices and apps.

As you implement your plan, remember that some changes might take some getting used to. For example, you might find it cumbersome initially to use a password manager or adjust to secure browsing practices. However, these habits will become more comfortable over time, and the security benefits they provide are well worth the effort.

7. Regularly Reviewing and Updating Your Plan

Cyber threats are continually evolving, so it is essential to regularly review and update your plan. Make a schedule to reassess your digital lifestyle, potential threats, and security goals at least once a year or whenever there is a significant change in your online behavior.

Also, stay informed about the latest cyber threats and cybersecurity practices. You can do this by following reputable tech news sites, cybersecurity blogs, and official government cybersecurity advisories.

8. Emergency Response

No matter how well-prepared you are, there is always a chance that you will become a victim of a cyber-attack. Include in your plan what steps you will take in the event of a security incident. This might include actions like contacting your bank if your financial information is compromised, reporting identity theft to the appropriate authorities, or taking your device to a professional if it is infected with malware.

Conclusion

Creating a comprehensive cybersecurity plan can seem like a daunting task, but it is an essential step towards protecting yourself in the digital world. Your plan will serve as a roadmap guiding you on what actions to take, when to take them, and how to respond if something goes wrong. Remember, cybersecurity is not a set-and-forget task - it requires continuous effort and vigilance.

By understanding the principles of cybersecurity, implementing best practices, using effective tools, and having a dynamic and robust cybersecurity plan, you will be well-equipped to protect your digital life. Continue to stay informed, stay vigilant, and above all, stay secure.

CHAPTER 11: SUMMARY OF THE BEST PERSONAL CYBERSECURITY PRACTICES

As we have seen throughout this guide, personal cybersecurity is an expansive and ever-evolving subject. It involves understanding threats, managing your digital lifestyle securely, implementing robust measures to protect your devices, and continuously updating your knowledge and practices. In this final chapter, we will summarize the key points that we have covered to offer a concise, easy-to-follow reference for the best personal cybersecurity practices.

1. Understand Cybersecurity and Potential Threats

Awareness is the first step towards effective cybersecurity. You should understand the various types of threats (like malware, phishing, and identity theft) and how they can impact your digital life. Also, be aware of the mechanisms by which these threats can infiltrate your system, like through suspicious emails, insecure websites, or unsecured networks.

2. Use Strong, Unique Passwords

Every online account should have a strong, unique password. Use a mix of letters, numbers, and special characters and avoid using obvious information like names or birthdays. A password manager can help manage your passwords securely and make it easier to use complex passwords.

3. Enable Two-Factor Authentication (2FA)

Wherever possible, enable 2FA for your online accounts. This adds an extra layer of security by requiring a second form of authentication, typically a code sent to your phone or generated by an app.

4. Keep Software and Systems Updated

Updates often include patches for security vulnerabilities, so it is essential to keep your operating system, apps, and devices updated. Turn on automatic updates wherever possible.

5. Secure Your Web Browsing

Use secure connections (https://), be cautious when downloading files or clicking on links, and consider using a VPN, especially when using public Wi-Fi. Additionally, regularly clear your browsing data and use privacy-oriented web browsers and search engines.

6. Secure Your Email

Be wary of unsolicited emails, especially those that ask for personal information or prompt you to click on a link or download a file. Use email filtering options and spam blockers to filter out potential threats.

7. Be Smart on Social Media

Limit the amount of personal information you share on social media, use privacy settings to control who can see your content, and be cautious of friend requests or messages from strangers.

8. Secure Your Mobile Devices

Use a screen lock, regularly update your apps and operating system, only download apps from trusted sources, and be careful when granting app permissions.

9. Protect Your Personal Data

Be mindful of where and how you share personal information. Use encryption for sensitive data, and safely dispose of old devices and data.

10. Shop Online Safely

Only shop from secure and reputable websites, use secure payment methods, and keep an eye on your financial statements for any unusual activity.

11. Use Antivirus Software

Install a reputable antivirus program on your devices and keep it updated. Regularly perform scans and address any threats promptly.

12. Create and Implement a Cybersecurity Plan

Assess your digital lifestyle, identify potential threats, set security goals, and develop a plan to improve your personal cybersecurity. This plan should be reviewed and updated regularly.

Cybersecurity is a journey rather than a destination. As technology and cyber threats continue to evolve, so must our approach to cybersecurity. Remember to stay informed about the latest threats and cybersecurity practices, and maintain a proactive stance towards your online safety. Your efforts in maintaining strong personal cybersecurity practices not only protect you but contribute to the broader effort of creating a safer digital world for everyone.

DISCLAIMER

As always, the advice of a competent professional should be sought. The author and publisher do not warrant the performance, effectiveness or applicability of any sites listed or linked to in this report. All links are for information purposes only and are not warranted for content, accuracy or any other implied or explicit purpose.

COPYRIGHT